Original title:
Finding Home

Copyright © 2024 Swan Charm
All rights reserved.

Author: Liina Liblikas
ISBN HARDBACK: 978-9916-89-898-7
ISBN PAPERBACK: 978-9916-89-899-4
ISBN EBOOK: 978-9916-89-900-7

# **The Pilgrim's Embrace**

In shadows deep, the journey starts,
A heart pours forth its silent pleas.
With weary feet and trembling spark,
The path unfolds like ancient trees.

Each step divine, a whisper calls,
To find the grace in each new dawn.
Through storms and trials, the spirit stalls,
Yet finds the peace of heaven's lawn.

The road is long, but faith will guide,
Through valleys low and mountains high.
In every tear, a hope resides,
The pilgrim's way will never die.

## Sanctuary of the Soul

Within the walls of silent prayer,
The soul finds solace, pure and bright.
A sacred space, devoid of care,
In quietude, it seeks the light.

The altar built of love and grace,
Resounds with echoes of the past.
Each whispered word, a warm embrace,
In unity, our shadows cast.

The heart's confessions softly rise,
As angels gather round the flame.
A melody that never dies,
In sanctuary, we are the same.

## Illuminated Pathways

Through veils of dusk, the stars appear,
A luminous guide for hearts in quest.
With faith as light, we cast out fear,
On sacred trails, our spirits rest.

Each twist and turn, a lesson learned,
In shadows' dance, the truth revealed.
The power of love forever burned,
In every step, our wounds are healed.

So follow where the light may lead,
With open hearts and hands outstretched.
In every moment, plant the seed,
For life is love, and love is etched.

## The Embrace of Eternity

In silence deep, the cosmos sings,
A tapestry of endless grace.
The joy it brings, like gentle wings,
Cradles us in its warm embrace.

With every heartbeat, time unfolds,
A bridge to realms both near and far.
In stories told, the truth beholds,
Eternity, our guiding star.

As moments fade, our spirits soar,
In love's embrace, we find our way.
Together bound forevermore,
In endless night and brightening day.

## Reflection in the Water's Edge

In stillness, I gaze at the surface bright,
Where ripples whisper a soft, golden light.
I seek His presence, calm and divine,
In the sacred mirror, my heart intertwines.

The echoes of prayer, they dance in the air,
A melody carried, so gentle, so rare.
The waters reflect each hope and each fear,
As I cast my burdens, He draws ever near.

With every wave, I find strength to renew,
His love like a river, steadfast and true.
In the depths, I surrender my soul to His grace,
Grateful for love in this hallowed place.

Beneath the vast heavens, I feel His embrace,
The beauty of nature, a sacred space.
Oh, let my spirit flow free like the stream,
In the reflection, I find hope's gentle gleam.

As twilight descends, I whisper my plea,
For wisdom and peace, a divine decree.
In the silence, I know His whispers will guide,
In the water's reflection, my spirit abides.

## Emissary of Love's Harbor

In the heart of the storm, love gathers its strength,
An emissary sent, boundless in length.
With arms wide open, it welcomes the lost,
In each kind embrace, we measure the cost.

Through trials of life, the beacon will shine,
A harbor of hope, a gift so divine.
It beckons the weary, the broken, the frail,
With whispers of faith that shall never pale.

In the depths of despair, a glimmer appears,
A soft, steady warmth to silence our fears.
Love's harbor is rich; it holds every dream,
A sanctuary, safe, like a sunlit stream.

With each gentle wave, we rise and we fall,
Yet love keeps us anchored, through it all.
In the vastness of skies, our spirits will soar,
As emissaries of love, we open the door.

So come, take my hand in this sacred quest,
Together we'll find solace, peace, and rest.
For in the embrace of compassion we thrive,
In love's harbor, we're truly alive.

## The Altar of Solace

In quiet corners, grace resides,
Where whispers of the spirit glide.
A sanctuary, soft and bright,
It offers peace in darkest night.

On humble stone, prayers are cast,
Each plea a bridge, each moment vast.
In solace found, our hearts unfold,
A tapestry of faith retold.

Within the stillness, hope renews,
The soul embraced by sacred views.
With every tear, a seed is sown,
In love's embrace, we find our home.

## Beneath Heaven's Canopy

Beneath the stars, where dreams take flight,
In nature's arms, all feels so right.
The heavens arch with gentle grace,
Awakening the spirit's place.

With every breeze, a promise made,
In sunlight's warmth, our fears do fade.
A whisper echoes through the trees,
A song of life, the soul's reprise.

Through trials faced, we rise anew,
In love's embrace, our path is true.
No shadows cast can dim our light,
For under heaven, hearts ignite.

## **The Divine Dwelling**

In every heart, a sacred space,
A dwelling place of boundless grace.
The spirit moves, a gentle flow,
In tender moments, love will grow.

Through winding paths, we seek the flame,
In quietude, we find our name.
The walls of hope, we build with care,
In prayerful silence, we are bare.

Here, kindness blooms like evening's rose,
In unity, the spirit knows.
The divine spark in all we share,
A gift of love, beyond compare.

## **Where Love Cultivates**

In fields of joy, where love is sown,
The heart finds now its truest home.
With every act of kindness shown,
The seeds of grace, we have outgrown.

Beneath the sun, our spirits dance,
In every glance, a fleeting chance.
To cultivate what lives inside,
In tender hearts, our dreams abide.

The rising dawn paints skies anew,
In warmth of love, our sorrows do.
Together, hand in hand we grow,
In this embrace, our spirits glow.

## A Journey Into Divine Embrace

In the stillness of morning light,
We seek the grace, our spirits bright.
With every step on sacred ground,
In whispers soft, His voice is found.

Through valleys deep and mountains high,
We wander forth, our hearts reply.
Each challenge faced, a lesson learned,
In faith, our flames of love are burned.

The path ahead seems dimly lit,
But trust in Him, we shall not quit.
For hand in hand, we walk the way,
In every dawn, the promise stays.

With every prayer, our souls unite,
In darkness deep, we find the light.
The waters clear, the skies above,
We journey forth, embraced in love.

At journey's end, the peace we find,
In unity, our hearts aligned.
Eternal love, our guiding grace,
In every breath, His warm embrace.

## Gathering Light in the Shadows

In twilight's hush, we gather round,
In shadows deep, the lost are found.
With every whisper, hope ignites,
We share the warmth, our hearts take flight.

The gentle night, a cloak of grace,
In every soul, a sacred space.
The stars above, they softly gleam,
In unity, we dare to dream.

When burdens weigh, and spirits wane,
We lift each other through the pain.
Each tear that falls, a diamond bright,
In gathering love, we find the light.

Through trials fierce, together stand,
In faith, we form a mighty band.
With arms outstretched, we boldly face,
The shadows fall, replaced by grace.

In morning's dawn, we rise anew,
With hearts ablaze, we chase the true.
For light we gather, hand in hand,
In every heart, a promised land.

## In the Garden of Resplendence

In gardens lush where flowers bloom,
The fragrance sweet dispels the gloom.
With open hearts, we tend the soil,
In harmony, we share the toil.

The radiant sun, a guiding star,
Illuminates our way from far.
In every petal, love's embrace,
We find the joy, the sacred space.

Through gentle rains, our spirits grow,
With every drop, we come to know.
The seeds of faith we plant today,
Shall yield the blessings on our way.

In moments still, the whispers call,
In unity, we rise and fall.
With every laugh and every tear,
We gather strength, dispelling fear.

In this garden, we belong,
A vibrant chorus, a hopeful song.
In resplendence, our spirits soar,
In love's embrace, forevermore.

## An Invocation of the Heart's Refuge

In silence deep, we seek the light,
With humble hearts, we take our flight.
In prayerful whispers, souls align,
This sacred space, where love shall shine.

From every wound, a lesson grows,
In every silence, truth bestows.
The heart's refuge, a gentle grace,
In trials faced, we seek His face.

An invocation, soft and clear,
In faith we gather, drawing near.
With every breath, our spirits blend,
In love's embrace, all shall mend.

Through trials met, and storms we brave,
In every moment, His love we crave.
Together bound, we rise above,
This sacred place, our home of love.

In unity, our voices sing,
From hearts set free, a new dawn brings.
In refuge found, we claim our part,
In every beat, a grateful heart.

## Abode of Angels

In realms where light eternal glows,
The angels dance in pure repose.
Their whispers soft, like breezes fair,
They lift our souls in silent prayer.

With wings of grace they soar above,
In every heart, a tale of love.
Through trials faced, they guard our way,
Their presence brightens darkest day.

A haven found in faith's embrace,
Where mercy shines and time finds peace.
The sacred songs, we hum along,
In the abode where all belong.

Oh, let us seek this holy place,
Where sorrow turns to sweetened grace.
In every step, the angels guide,
Through paths of light, and heaven wide.

## The Heart's Refuge

Within the soul, a sacred space,
A refuge built of love and grace.
In storms that toss the restless sea,
The heart finds peace, it longs to be.

The whispers of divine embrace,
Fill every silent, empty place.
Here fears dissolve, and doubts take flight,
A gentle warmth, the purest light.

Each prayer a seed in fertile ground,
In quietude, the truth is found.
With every heartbeat, hope will rise,
A sacred bond that harmonizes.

So in the stillness, seek and trust,
In love's protection, we are thrust.
A place where faith and courage blend,
The heart's refuge will never end.

**A Tapestry of Grace**

In every thread, a tale unfolds,
A tapestry where faith upholds.
Each color rich, with purpose spun,
A sacred weave, where hearts are one.

Through trials faced and joys embraced,
The fabric sings of love's sweet grace.
In darkness' shadow, light appears,
A woven bond that calms our fears.

Each stitch a prayer, each knot a vow,
In unity, we learn to bow.
With hands extended, we shall share,
The tapestry of hope and care.

In sacred circles, threads entwine,
Together woven, souls divine.
With every heartbeat, we proclaim,
In love's rich fabric, none are the same.

## Paths of the Pilgrim

We wander forth on sacred ground,
With every step, a truth profound.
The road is long, the journey wide,
Yet faith guides us, our steadfast guide.

Through valleys low and mountains high,
In every tear, a silent cry.
The stars above, our compass bright,
Illuminate the paths of light.

Each pilgrim soul, a story shared,
In heart's embrace, we are declared.
Together bound by love's embrace,
We tread with hope on sacred space.

With every dawn, we rise anew,
In sacred trust, our strength imbue.
The paths we walk, though hard and steep,
In faith's promise, our souls shall leap.

## **The Hearth of Hope**

In the quiet glow of faith's warm light,
Hearts gather close, banishing night.
With whispered prayers in softest tones,
The embers of hope ignite our bones.

Through trials faced and burdens borne,
We rise anew, a mantle worn.
In every tear, a lesson clear,
The hearth of hope draws us near.

We share our dreams with open hands,
Together we stand, in love's commands.
A single flame to chase the dark,
In unity's name, we leave our mark.

With gentle hearts, we mend the fray,
Lighting the path, come what may.
In the quiet moments, we find our way,
The hearth of hope, where spirits sway.

## Celestial Foundations

Stars above in a sacred dance,
Whisper secrets in a cosmic trance.
The moonlight drapes our weary souls,
Guiding us through life's many scrolls.

From distant realms, the angels sing,
Carrying peace on gentle wing.
With every note, a promise shared,
In celestial foundations, we are prepared.

The sun arises, bright and bold,
A reminder of stories yet to be told.
In each dawn, a chance to start,
To weave the threads of the faithful heart.

With faith as our anchor, we must trust,
In divine designs, in boundless love.
Each step we take, a sacred sound,
In the dance of life, we are tightly bound.

## The Embrace of Compassion

In the stillness of a welcoming heart,
We gather close, never apart.
Each gentle touch, a soothing balm,
In the embrace of compassion, we find calm.

With open arms, we welcome grace,
In the eyes of others, we see a trace.
Of struggles faced and battles won,
Together united, we are one.

In kindness woven, we cast our net,
Catching dreams that we won't forget.
Through every storm, we share the weight,
In compassion's light, we elevate.

When shadows fall, and hearts grow cold,
Compassion's story will be told.
Through every tear, we find renewal,
In love's embrace, life's sacred fuel.

## The Harbor of Harmony

In the harbor where souls unite,
We find solace, pure and bright.
With gentle waves that kiss the shore,
Harmony sings forevermore.

Boats of faith sail side by side,
In this safe space, we confide.
Through every storm, we hold our ground,
In the harbor of harmony, love abounds.

With every word, a melody shared,
In unity's grip, we are prepared.
To face the tides that life can send,
In the embrace of friendship, we transcend.

As sun and moon each take their turn,
In this safe harbor, our spirits burn.
Together we stand, unwavering and free,
In the harbor of harmony, we shall be.

## **Embracing the Eternal Journey**

In the stillness of dawn's glow,
We gather our thoughts like the flow.
With each step on this sacred ground,
Wisdom whispers softly, profound.

Hearts open wide to the divine,
Through trials faced, our souls align.
The horizon stretches, vast and bright,
In faith, we walk towards the light.

Every moment a gift we hold,
In the tapestry of stories told.
With hands united, spirits soar,
Together we seek, forevermore.

Through valleys deep, we find our way,
Guided by stars that gently sway.
The journey calls, a sacred quest,
In love's embrace, we find our rest.

With each heartbeat, a sacred hymn,
In the dance of life, we learn to swim.
With open arms, we greet the day,
Embracing light along the way.

## **Walls Built of Light**

In a world of shadows and fears,
We raise our voices, wipe our tears.
With faith as our shield, we unite,
Building walls that glow with light.

Kindness and love, our strong decree,
In hearts entwined, we find a plea.
Each brick a prayer, each smile a spark,
Illuminating pathways in the dark.

Together we stand, hand in hand,
Creating a fortress, forever grand.
Embraced by warmth, we shine so bright,
In harmony's glow, we banish night.

With grace, we mend the broken seams,
Turning pain into radiant dreams.
In the fortress of love, we abide,
These walls built of light, our sacred guide.

Through the storms that may come our way,
We trust in the dawn of a new day.
In unity's kiss, we find our might,
These walls will hold, forever in light.

## A Hearth of Healing

By the fire's glow, we gather near,
In the warmth, we shed our fear.
Each word a balm, each touch a grace,
In this circle, we find our place.

Laughter echoes, a sacred sound,
In this hearth, our hearts are found.
With stories shared, our spirits mend,
In love's embrace, we all transcend.

Through trials faced, we grow and learn,
In the flickering flames, our passions burn.
A tapestry woven with care and hope,
In this space, together we cope.

With compassion's light to guide our way,
We heal the wounds of yesterday.
In the warmth of trust, we open wide,
This hearth of healing, our sacred tide.

As embers glow and shadows dance,
In unity, we find our chance.
With each heartbeat, we forge anew,
A hearth of love, forever true.

## The Voice of the Divine

In whispers soft, the spirit speaks,
Through rustling leaves, the heart seeks.
A symphony of love, profound,
In every moment, grace is found.

In the stillness, a gentle call,
Reminding us, we're not alone at all.
The voice of the divine guides our way,
Illuminating paths, come what may.

In laughter and tears, it weaves a song,
In every heartbeat, we all belong.
With open ears, we listen well,
To the sacred truths, our hearts compel.

With faith as our compass, we align,
In the sacred dance, we intertwine.
Each step a prayer, a rhythm so true,
The voice of the divine sings anew.

In shadows cast and light bestowed,
We tread the sacred, humble road.
With gratitude, we lift our praise,
To the voice of the divine, always.

## **Where the Wanderers Meet**

In the stillness, hearts unite,
Journeying souls in the twilight,
Each path winding, a sacred thread,
Guided by grace where angels tread.

In the circle, stories unfold,
Whispers of wisdom, ages old,
With open hands and spirits free,
Together we find our destiny.

Beneath the stars, a shared embrace,
In every smile, a holy space,
As wanderers seek and often roam,
They find in love their sacred home.

With every prayer, the air ignites,
Bound by truth, in faith's delights,
In unity, we break the night,
Where wanderers meet, the world feels right.

So let us gather, hand in hand,
In the light of a holy land,
Together, forever, let us be,
Where wanderers meet, eternally.

## Symphony of a Sacred Return

In the hush of dawn's sweet light,
We gather in love's pure sight,
Voices rise, a gentle hymn,
Guided home as spirits swim.

Each note a prayer, a soft embrace,
Melodies woven of sacred grace,
In the chamber of the heart's refrain,
We find our strength through joy and pain.

With every step, the rhythm pounds,
In the quiet, truth resounds,
A symphony of the soul's deep yearn,
In harmonious love, we learn.

Through valleys low and mountains high,
The sacred call, a sweet lullaby,
As we wander through valleys of doubt,
With faith in each note, we sing out.

So let the chords of love resound,
In every heart, let grace abound,
In this symphony, we all belong,
A sacred return, forever strong.

## The Homeward Pilgrimage

Upon the road where shadows lay,
We walk in light at break of day,
With every step our spirits soar,
In the longing for home, we explore.

The path is stained with tears and joys,
Of faith untouched, the soul employs,
With whispered prayers, we clear the way,
In the heart's embrace, we choose to stay.

Through valleys dim, and hills so vast,
Our hearts beat loud, the die is cast,
In the journey's dance, we find our grace,
In love's warm light, we see His face.

As stars above guide our plight,
In every moment, shines His light,
The pilgrimage leads to love's sweet shore,
In unity, we are forevermore.

So raise your hands, the call is clear,
Homeward we go, without fear,
Together we march, strong and bright,
On the homeward pilgrimage, hearts alight.

# **Celestial Whispers of Togetherness**

In the quiet, a voice is heard,
Whispers of love, a sacred word,
Under the arch of heaven's grace,
Together we seek a holy space.

Through open skies, our spirits blend,
In celestial songs, we find a friend,
As stars align in bright array,
We grasp the night, to greet the day.

With every tear, a story sown,
In laughter shared, we're never alone,
The harmony of hearts in flight,
Brings us closer, a wondrous sight.

In the tapestry of kindness spun,
Each thread a heart, we're all as one,
With open hearts and hands to give,
Together we breathe, together we live.

So let us gather in sacred space,
In celestial whispers, find our place,
With love as our guide, forever blessed,
In togetherness, we find our rest.

**Wings of Compassion**

In shadows deep, a whisper calls,
With wings of mercy, love enthralls.
Each heart a spark, in darkness bright,
Guided by grace, we find the light.

With open arms, we share our gifts,
Through storms of sorrow, the spirit lifts.
In quiet moments, kindness grows,
Together we rise, as hope bestows.

From every tear, a lesson learned,
In every heart, compassion burned.
The gentle touch, of soothing balm,
Restores the spirit, brings the calm.

So let us soar, on faith's embrace,
With wings that wrap the weary space.
In every step, remember this:
Compassion's path leads us to bliss.

Through trials faced, we stand as one,
Beneath the vast and radiant sun.
With hearts aligned, we cultivate,
A world of love, we recreate.

## Sanctuary of the Soul

In silence vast, the spirit speaks,
A sanctuary, solace seeks.
With open doors, where kindness dwells,
In sacred peace, the heart compels.

Each whispered prayer, a gentle touch,
The soul finds refuge, oh so much.
Within these walls, pure love abides,
In every breath, the spirit guides.

Through trials faced, we gather near,
In unity, we cast our fear.
A haven warm, where hope ignites,
Together shining through the nights.

With every heart, a sacred flame,
In this embrace, we find our name.
A family bound by faith's decree,
In sanctuary, we learn to be.

Let every soul, its truth unfold,
In love and light, our hearts are bold.
The journey shared, no path too long,
In this haven, we find our song.

**Pilgrimage to the Heart's Haven**

With every step, the journey calls,
To sacred places, where spirit enthralls.
Through valleys low, and mountains high,
In search of truth, we lift our eyes.

The road is long, the path unclear,
Yet faith, it lights the way, my dear.
In every heartbeat, a compass clear,
Guided by love, we banish fear.

With every dawn, new hope we find,
In pilgrims' hearts, a thread entwined.
Through trials faced, we grow so strong,
Together in faith, we all belong.

In sacred spaces, we pause and pray,
For strength to guide us on our way.
In every moment, grace bestows,
A love divine, that ever flows.

And as we walk, let spirits soar,
In heart's haven, forevermore.
For in this quest, we know it true,
Our pilgrimage leads us to You.

## The Embrace of Familiar Shores

Upon the shores of memory's tide,
In familiar embrace, we abide.
Each wave that crashes sings the song,
Of love and faith, where we belong.

Beneath the sky, so vast and blue,
In gentle whispers, the truth shines through.
The comfort found in every breath,
A shelter strong, beyond all death.

Each moment spent, a treasure dear,
In every laugh, we conquer fear.
Hand in hand, we face the storm,
In love's embrace, we are reborn.

With every tide, a promise made,
Through trials faced, we will not fade.
In unity, our spirits soar,
With open hearts, we seek for more.

So here we stand on sacred ground,
In familiar shores, love knows no bound.
Together, wise, we chart our course,
In every heart, a sacred source.

## The Altar of Nowhere

In the silence of the void, we kneel,
Seeking truths that we can feel.
Whispers rise from barren ground,
In the darkness, light is found.

Sacred rituals of the night,
Guide our hearts towards the light.
Hands outstretched, we long to see,
The grace that sets our spirits free.

Altar built with dreams and fears,
Carved with hopes and shaped by tears.
Each moment holds a holy spark,
Illuminating paths through dark.

Where faith and doubt collide and weave,
In the stillness, we believe.
Visions dance on edges blurred,
In the silence, truth is stirred.

From nowhere springs a sacred flow,
An essence only hearts may know.
With souls aligned, we hear the call,
In the void, we find it all.

**Wandering to the Divine Nest**

Wandering paths with weary feet,
Seeking solace, pure and sweet.
In the forest, whispers guide,
To the nest where hopes abide.

Branches bend with tales untold,
Cocoon of warmth in arms of gold.
In the shadows, secrets bloom,
Carried gently, dispelling gloom.

Breath of spirit fills the air,
In each heartbeat, echoes rare.
Infinite love enfolds us tight,
As day yields to the embrace of night.

In stillness, we find our place,
Nestled deep in endless grace.
Each moment a divine caress,
A journey wrapped in tenderness.

From the depths of heart's desire,
We kindle soft, the sacred fire.
Wandering souls, hand in hand,
Finding peace in promised land.

## **Where the Spirit Rests**

In the meadow's gentle sway,
Where the spirit finds its way.
Softly held by nature's breath,
Cradled close to life and death.

Time stands still, a sacred pause,
In the stillness, holy laws.
Waves of calm caress the soul,
Mending pieces, making whole.

Beneath the sky's celestial dome,
Here, every heart can find a home.
Whispers of the past resound,
In this sacred space unbound.

From the earth, the spirit soars,
Through the infinite, love explores.
In the quiet, truth concedes,
Hidden within our deepest needs.

As twilight wraps us in its light,
Where the spirit takes delight.
Embracing all that life imparts,
In every breath, the sacred starts.

## Holy Echoes of the Hearth

In the warmth of flame and kindled light,
Holy echoes pierce the night.
Voices rise like smoke to sky,
Gathering dreams that never die.

The hearth, a cradle for our prayer,
Holding stories beyond compare.
With each flicker, spirits dance,
In the shadows, we find our chance.

Gathered round, hearts open wide,
In this circle, there's no pride.
Each confession, a step towards grace,
In the light, we find our place.

Beyond the flame, the world fades,
In our souls, the truth cascades.
Peace descends like gentle rain,
Washing over every pain.

Holy echoes, a timeless song,
Binding us, where we belong.
With every laugh and tear we share,
In this love, we find our prayer.

## Cloaked in Celestial Peace

In quiet moments, mercy falls,
As whispers weave through sacred halls.
Hearts embraced by grace so pure,
In love's embrace, we find our cure.

Beneath the stars, our spirits soar,
Guided by light forevermore.
In stillness found, the soul will learn,
With every breath, for Him, we yearn.

Each prayer a thread in heaven's loom,
We seek the light to banish gloom.
In sacred silence, joy ignites,
A dance of faith in holy sights.

As the dawn breaks, shadows flee,
In every heartbeat, we are free.
Cloaked in peace, we rise anew,
In love divine, our spirits grew.

And in the night, when doubt prevails,
Hope's gentle whisper surely sails.
United we stand, in realms so vast,
Where every soul, in grace, is cast.

**The Sacred Nest**

In quietude, the heart resides,
Within the nest where faith abides.
Softly cradled, love unfolds,
A story of grace, sacredly told.

Feathers of hope line every wall,
In unity's embrace, we stand tall.
A shelter made of cherished dreams,
Reflecting light in gentle beams.

Hands held high in gratitude,
For blessings shared, a sacred mood.
In every laugh, in every tear,
The nest of love draws us near.

When trials come like stormy seas,
We find our strength in sacred pleas.
In the warmth of the nest, we stay,
Together we'll rise, come what may.

So let us build with tender care,
A refuge strong beyond compare.
In the sacred nest where spirits roam,
We find our path, we find our home.

## In the Shadow of the Divine

In the quiet shade, we seek the light,
The warmth that guides us through the night.
Veiled in grace, we walk the way,
In the shadow, hope will stay.

When burdens weigh upon our soul,
In whispered prayers, we seek the whole.
With faith as our anchor, hearts align,
In the vast embrace of the divine.

Upon the mountain, we lift our eyes,
To the heavens where love never dies.
In every moment, blessings flow,
In the shadow, peace will grow.

Hearts entwined in sacred song,
In unity, where we belong.
Through trials faced, we will rise,
In the shadow, love never lies.

So let us gather beneath the sky,
In the grace of Him, we learn to fly.
In the shadow of the divine we find,
A world of joy, forever kind.

## Shelter from the Storm

When the tempest rages, fierce and wild,
  We seek the refuge of the Child.
In sacred halls where hope takes flight,
  We find our peace, our guiding light.

  Each drop of rain a tear released,
  In every heart, the pain deceased.
  With open arms, the heavens call,
    In shelter sweet, we stand tall.

As thunder roars, and shadows play,
  We hold each other, come what may.
In the storm's embrace, we stand as one,
  With faith unbroken till the dawn.

In whispered prayers, the calm appears,
  Drying the sorrow, erasing fears.
The shelter strong, divine and pure,
  In love's embrace, we find our cure.

So let the winds howl, let the rains pour,
  In shelter's arms, we find our core.
With hearts united, fear disarms,
  In sacred love, we find our charms.

## The Covenant of Comfort

In the hush of dawn, we gather near,
With whispers of faith, we hold what's dear.
A promise of peace, a bond made strong,
In grace we walk, where hearts belong.

Through valleys low and mountains high,
His love envelops, like the sky.
In every trial, in every tear,
The covenant stands, to calm our fear.

We share our burdens, our sorrows bare,
In unity, we find His care.
Together we rise, through joy and strife,
In the covenant of comfort, we embrace life.

With every prayer, our spirits soar,
In the sacred space, we seek and implore.
With open hearts, His light we seek,
In the covenant's warmth, we are never weak.

So let the world around us fade,
In holy trust, our bond displayed.
For in His presence, we'll always stay,
The covenant gives strength, come what may.

## Havens of Hope

In every storm, a shelter stands,
With open arms and guiding hands.
A haven built on faith and love,
A gift bestowed from God above.

When shadows fall and spirits dim,
We look to Him, our hearts' hymn.
With light that shines through darkest night,
He leads us forward, in purest light.

Life's heavy burdens, we lay down,
In His grace, we lift our crown.
Among the faithful, we find our rest,
In havens of hope, we are truly blessed.

The weary traveler, find peace here,
In sacred whispers, casting fear.
Together we stand, our faith unshaken,
In every heart, a dream awakened.

As dawn unfolds with gentle plea,
We rise anew, with hearts set free.
In havens of hope, we dance and sing,
For in His love, we are everything.

## **Sunlight on Sacred Soil**

In gentle rays, the morning breaks,
On sacred soil, our spirit wakes.
With every bloom, a promise lies,
Beneath the heavens, our praises rise.

The earth we tread, blessed and pure,
In faith, we walk, our hearts secure.
With every step, a hymn we share,
In sunlight's warmth, we breathe the air.

Nature whispers, and we must heed,
The sacred call, for every need.
With open hearts, we hear the song,
In sunlight's glow, we all belong.

Through every season, our spirits grow,
In roots of love, our blessings flow.
With gratitude, we lift our voice,
In sunlight's grace, we rejoice.

So let us cherish, this sacred place,
Where God's love shines with tender grace.
On sacred soil, our bond will hold,
In sunlight's warmth, our faith unfolds.

## The Refuge of Serenity

In quiet moments, find thy peace,
Within His arms, all troubles cease.
A refuge found in faith's embrace,
In serenity, we seek His grace.

The world can roar, yet we remain,
In stillness deep, we break the chain.
With every breath, our spirits mend,
In refuge blessed, we find a friend.

Through trials fierce, our hearts hold fast,
In His gentle love, we are steadfast.
With open souls, we lean on Him,
In refuge pure, our light won't dim.

As rivers flow and seasons change,
His presence near, nothing feels strange.
In every heartbeat, His whisper flows,
In the refuge of serenity, our essence glows.

So let us dwell, where peace abides,
In tranquil shores, our faith resides.
In unity, we lift our voice,
For in serenity, we rejoice.

## **Sheltering Wings**

O Lord, in shadows deep we find,
Your wings enfold us, soft and kind.
In trials faced, we seek Your grace,
In every breath, we seek Your face.

From storms that rage, our hearts take flight,
Under Your shelter, all is right.
With faith our guide, we tread the way,
In Your embrace, we long to stay.

Through valleys low, we walk anew,
With every step, we trust in You.
Your love, a beacon, bright and clear,
In sheltering wings, we banish fear.

In whispered prayers, our souls unite,
In every moment, You are the light.
With gratitude, we lift our song,
In Your warm embrace, we all belong.

## The Sacred Hearth

In the heart of home, where love ignites,
We gather close on starry nights.
A sacred space, where spirits meet,
In gentle warmth, our lives are sweet.

With every flame, our fears dissolve,
In sacred hearth, our souls evolve.
Through trials faced, we find our strength,
In love's embrace, we go the length.

Come share a meal, let kindness reign,
In each embrace, we ease the pain.
Our laughter rings, a holy sound,
In sacred hearth, true love is found.

Around the fire, our stories blend,
In every heart, our spirits mend.
With gratitude, our voices rise,
In the sacred hearth, where love never dies.

## **Pilgrimage of the Heart**

Upon this path, we tread with care,
A pilgrimage of love and prayer.
With every step, we seek and yearn,
For wisdom found and hearts that burn.

In valleys low and mountains high,
We chase the stars, we touch the sky.
A journey guided by faith's embrace,
In every stumble, we find grace.

With open hearts, we share our fears,
In laughter shared, in whispered tears.
Together strong, we face the unknown,
In unity, our strength has grown.

Through every trial, our spirits rise,
In this pilgrimage, love never lies.
With every dawn, new hope takes flight,
Our hearts will guide us to the light.

## Beneath Divine Arches

Beneath the arches, angels sing,
A sanctuary, offering.
In whispered hymns, our spirits soar,
In quiet grace, our hearts explore.

With open hands, we seek to give,
In love's embrace, we learn to live.
Together bound, our souls entwined,
In sacred peace, our hearts aligned.

As light pours in, our fears diminish,
In every moment, hope will finish.
With faith as anchor, strong and clear,
Beneath divine arches, God is near.

We walk in trust, each step a prayer,
In every heart, love's gentle care.
United in faith, we'll find our way,
Beneath divine arches, we shall stay.

# Lanterns of Belonging

In shadows deep, the lanterns glow,
Guiding hearts where rivers flow.
Each flicker whispers, we are one,
A tapestry of faith begun.

Through valleys wide, we seek the light,
In every soul, a spark so bright.
Together we rise, hand in hand,
In love's embrace, forever stand.

With every step, we find our way,
In sacred trust, we choose to stay.
The bonds we share, a holy thread,
In joy and sorrow, love is spread.

As lanterns flicker in the night,
They share the warmth, a shared delight.
Compassion flows, unites our hearts,
In every ending, new life starts.

So let us walk this path as one,
With faith as bright as morning sun.
Together strong, we'll face the dawn,
In unity, we carry on.

# A Home in the Spirit

Within each heart, a sacred space,
Where kindness dwells, and love finds grace.
A sanctuary, strong and true,
A home in spirit, made for you.

In whispered prayers, our hopes align,
With every soul, the stars will shine.
Together we rise, like morning dew,
In trust and faith, we start anew.

Embracing all, both near and far,
In every heart, a guiding star.
The light of mercy gently pours,
Creating peace behind closed doors.

Through trials faced and joy we share,
In every moment, love declared.
A bond unbroken, ever strong,
In harmony, we'll sing our song.

So let us build this home of light,
Where spirit lifts, and shadows fight.
With open hearts, we'll find our way,
In love's embrace, forever stay.

## Soil of the Soul

In quiet earth, our roots run deep,
Where sacred trust, forever keeps.
Each tender seed, a dream begun,
In soil of soul, we are all one.

The storms may rage, the winds may howl,
But in the dark, we hear the fowl.
With gentle rain, our spirits quench,
As faith and hope begin to wrench.

In patient growth, our hearts will bloom,
In every shadow, love finds room.
Together we reach for the sun,
In unity, our work is spun.

With every dawn, the world awakes,
In harmony, our spirit shakes.
Together woven, threads of gold,
The stories of the brave retold.

So let the soil cradle our dreams,
In every heartbeat, nature seems.
In this embrace, we find our place,
In soil of soul, eternal grace.

## The Quietude of Faith

In whispers soft, the Spirit speaks,
In silent places, strength it seeks.
With every breath, a prayer takes flight,
In quietude, we find the light.

Through stillness profound, our hearts align,
In trust and hope, the worlds combine.
The gentle pause, a sacred call,
In unity, we rise, we fall.

In moments rare, we feel the grace,
A touch divine, a warm embrace.
With every step, we tread with care,
In gentle faith, our burdens share.

The echoes of love, forever near,
In quietude, we learn to hear.
Through trials faced, and joys embraced,
In solemn grace, our paths we traced.

So let us walk this road of peace,
In every heartbeat, find release.
With quietude, our spirits soar,
In gentle faith, forevermore.

# The Ancestral Echo of Loving

In shadows deep where whispers dwell,
Their love transcends, a sacred spell.
Through lifetimes past, their voices sing,
In every heart, their warmth they bring.

A tapestry of fate we weave,
With threads of faith, we must believe.
In every tear, a story flows,
In every joy, the ancients' glow.

With every prayer, their spirits rise,
In the quiet night, their laughter sighs.
Through valleys low and mountains high,
Their echoes dance in the boundless sky.

We gather here, a family blessed,
In love's embrace, we find our rest.
With open hearts, we honor the past,
In the circle of life, our bonds hold fast.

So let us walk this path of grace,
With loving hearts, our sacred place.
For in our souls, their legacy gleams,
Ancestral love, the heart's true dreams.

## Beneath the Watchful Stars

The heavens gleam with stories bright,
Each star a guide, a beacon of light.
Beneath this dome where shadows play,
We find our peace, we kneel and pray.

In silent night, our wishes soar,
To realms unknown, where spirits roar.
With every breath, we seek the grace,
That fills our hearts in this sacred space.

The moonlit path we dare to tread,
With faith in hearts, no fear or dread.
The cosmos sings a lullaby,
Of love divine, that will not die.

As night unfolds, our dreams take flight,
We trust in love, our guiding light.
With open souls, we dance and twirl,
Beneath the stars, together we whirl.

So let us cherish this gift of night,
In unity, hearts burning bright.
For in the silence, we are one,
Forever blessed by the holy sun.

## Gospel of the Wandering Heart

In search of truth, the heart will roam,
Through lands unknown, we seek a home.
With every step, a lesson learned,
With every flame, a passion burned.

The wandering soul knows no bound,
In quiet moments, grace is found.
From mountain high to valley low,
The gospel sings of love's bright glow.

With open eyes, we see the light,
That guides us through the darkest night.
In every trial, our spirits soar,
For love's embrace will ever bore.

Through tempest's roar and gentle breeze,
Our hearts will dance with sacred ease.
In every heartbeat, truth unfolds,
The wandering heart, its story told.

So let us tread this path of love,
With eyes on stars, and hearts above.
For every journey, though far apart,
Is blessed anew in the wandering heart.

## The Ethereal Call of Kindred Souls

In realms unseen, where spirits meet,
The call of kindred, pure and sweet.
With every breath, a bond we share,
In whispered prayers, we find our prayer.

Through shifting sands and timeless seas,
The ties unbroken, hearts at ease.
In every laugh, a memory flows,
In every tear, affection grows.

We gather 'round in sacred space,
In love's embrace, we find our place.
With open arms, we greet the day,
As light descends, our fears give way.

With gentle hearts, we weave our fate,
In trusting souls, we celebrate.
For in each other, we find the key,
Unlocking doors to eternity.

So let us sing this song of grace,
With every note, we sense His face.
For in this world, so vast and whole,
We find our home in kindred souls.

## Where Grace Encircles

In the stillness of the night,
Whispers weave through prayer's light.
Heaven's calm descends like dew,
Cradling the heart, so pure, so true.

Beneath the stars, hope brightly glows,
A beacon where the spirit flows.
Grace encircles, tender and wide,
In weary souls, it will abide.

Gentle hands guide each faltering,
In shadows where our fears are king.
Faith ignites a flame divine,
In the lost, a love will shine.

In every tear, a promise found,
With grace and mercy, we're unbound.
Oh, to be held in soft embrace,
Ever anchored, in grace, we trace.

Among the trials, storms may rise,
Yet in His arms, a sweet surprise.
For where grace flows, hope cannot cease,
In every heart, a touch of peace.

## Emblems of Eternity

In the tapestry of time so vast,
Emblems shine, our souls amassed.
Threads of faith weave through the night,
Glimmers of truth in Heaven's light.

Each prayer, a step on sacred ground,
With angels gathered all around.
Every heartbeat sings a tune,
A melody, divine, in bloom.

Eternity whispers in silence clear,
Calling us closer, dispelling fear.
In every choice, love's gentle guide,
Through the valleys, the Lord abides.

With every dawn, new life bestowed,
In the journey, our hearts have flowed.
Emblems of grace, in light they shine,
In the circle of love, divine.

On mountains high, or valleys low,
His promise rings, a constant glow.
In every moment, His presence near,
Emblems of eternity, crystal clear.

## The Heart's Sacred Embrace

In quiet moments, hearts entwined,
A sacred bond, forever defined.
With each breath, the spirit stirs,
In tenderness, true love occurs.

Veils of doubt begin to fade,
As faith and trust, together laid.
In the stillness, grace ignites,
The heart's embrace, the soul's delights.

Through trials faced, we rise anew,
With every challenge, stronger too.
In love we grow, in light we stand,
Together held by His own hand.

As seasons change and rivers flow,
In sacred joys, our spirits grow.
The heart knows well, by grace we live,
In every moment, love we give.

In laughter shared, in tears we find,
A glimpse of heaven, pure and kind.
The heart's embrace, a promise sealed,
In love's perfection, we are healed.

## Dimensions of Faith

In the silence of the soul, we seek,
Dimensions vast, through humble meek.
Faith that soars on wings of grace,
In every heart, a sacred space.

Journeying through both night and day,
With every step, we find our way.
In storms that rage, in peace that flows,
Faith, a river that gently grows.

With open hands, we reach for light,
The flame of hope, burning bright.
In whispers soft, the truth unfold,
In every story, faith retold.

Through aging hands and weary eyes,
We grasp the stars that fill the skies.
In moments still, His presence felt,
In every heart, our spirits melt.

The path of faith, winding and long,
Is filled with trials, yet makes us strong.
In every laugh, in every tear,
Dimensions of faith draw us near.

## Echoes of Eden's Embrace

In the garden's tender light,
Where whispers weave through leaves,
The heart finds peace in stillness,
In divinity, the spirit breathes.

Each petal tells a tale of grace,
A song of love, a sweet refrain,
In every shadow, hope awakes,
In every tear, a path to gain.

Morning dew like blessings fall,
Anointing faith with sacred tears,
Hearts entwined, we heed the call,
Casting out our worldly fears.

In unity, we lift our hands,
To skies that paint a vivid dawn,
Together walk this hallowed land,
With strength of spirit ever drawn.

Let echoes of this Eden sing,
In every soul, the light shall bloom,
A promise held, our offering,
In love, forever, we find room.

## A Covenant with the Soul's Horizon

In twilight's glow, a vow is made,
To seek the truth beyond the veil,
With every step, the heart cascades,
  A journey vast, a sacred trail.

Through tempest's rage and gentle nights,
  We wander forth, hand in hand,
Each star a guide, each dream ignites,
The flame of hope in this vast land.

In silence speaks the whispered prayer,
A promise sealed with love's embrace,
  In every soul, a purpose fair,
In faith, we find our rightful place.

The horizon calls with gentle breath,
A covenant forged in spirit's glow,
In life and death, in love's bequest,
  Together, we shall surely grow.

With hearts upturned, we seek the light,
  Through every shadow, every fear,
For in this bond we find our sight,
  Our souls united, ever near.

## Hearthstones of Eternal Kinship

Gathered close around the fire,
We share our stories, ancient tales,
In warmth, our spirits draw up higher,
Through laughter's grace, our love prevails.

Each hearthstone holds a memory,
A bond that time cannot erase,
In unity, a symphony,
Of kindred souls, a sacred space.

Through trials faced, hand in hand,
In joy and sorrow, we abide,
Together we shall ever stand,
Our faith, a bridge, our hearts, a guide.

In twilight's glow, our voices blend,
A hymn to love, a song of peace,
With each heartbeat, we transcend,
In kinship's light, our souls release.

So let the flames of trust arise,
Forever binding, strong and true,
In the hearth of love, our prize,
Eternal kinship, me and you.

## The Worn Path of Belief

Upon this road, the footsteps tread,
A journey old, yet ever new,
With every stone, the heart has bled,
The faith we carry lights our view.

Through valleys deep and mountains high,
We walk with purpose, hand in hand,
The heavens speak, the spirits sigh,
In every prayer, in every strand.

The sun will rise, and shadows flee,
As we embrace the trials faced,
In love, in grace, we strive to be,
The echoes of the past, interlaced.

In sacred whispers, wisdom calls,
The path ahead, though worn and bare,
With every stumble, the spirit thralls,
In unity, we rise, we dare.

So let us tread this path with care,
For every step, a chance to heal,
In faith, we find the strength to share,
The love that time cannot conceal.

# **Inhabitants of the Infinite**

In the silence of the stars, we find,
A whisper of the divine, intertwined.
Each heartbeat a prayer, fleeting yet bold,
In the vastness, our spirits unfold.

Guided by light from realms above,
We dance in the grace, wrapped in love.
The cosmos sings a celestial song,
Inhabitants of the infinite, we belong.

From the depths of night to dawn's embrace,
We seek the Creator, face to face.
In every shadow, in every gleam,
Dwells the promise of hope, like a dream.

We journey together, hand in hand,
Through valleys of faith, across sacred land.
Each step a testament, a choice to believe,
In the boundless compassion, we receive.

As souls take flight on wings of prayer,
We rise above the burdens we bear.
In the tapestry woven with threads of grace,
Inhabitants of the infinite, we find our place.

## The Whisper of Ancient Walls

Within the silence, stories reside,
Echoes of faith, where shadows abide.
Ancient walls hold the weight of dreams,
Whispers of truth flow in gentle streams.

In the sacred spaces, time stands still,
Each corner reflects the divine will.
Beneath the arches, hopes intertwine,
Sacred moments, transcending the line.

The footsteps of seekers, dust on the floor,
Journey unending, forever explore.
In the glow of candles, prayers ascend,
The whisper of ancient walls shall never end.

Each stone a witness, each crack a sigh,
In the embrace of eternity, we fly.
Here, we gather, hearts open wide,
Among the echoes, forever to bide.

We carry the warmth of those who have past,
A legacy of love in each breath cast.
In every silence, remember the call,
The divine in the hush of ancient walls.

## Psalms of Belonging

In the garden of souls, we all partake,
Unity in diversity, a world we make.
With hearts entwined, we sing our song,
Psalms of belonging, where we all belong.

Each note a promise, each word a light,
Illuminating pathways through the night.
Together we rise, together we share,
In the embrace of love, we find our care.

From distant shores to the mountains high,
We reach for the heavens, hand in hand, we try.
In laughter and tears, the bonds grow strong,
Psalms of belonging, where we all belong.

The tapestry woven with colors bright,
A masterpiece born from the depths of night.
In the circle of life, we celebrate song,
Together we thrive, where we all belong.

In every sunset, in each dawn's glow,
The spirit of unity continues to flow.
Let hearts be open, let praises prolong,
Psalms of belonging, in harmony, we throng.

**Serene Sanctuaries**

In quiet corners, peace does reside,
Serene sanctuaries where spirits abide.
Each whisper of wind carries a prayer,
In the stillness of heart, His presence is there.

Amidst the chaos, a refuge we find,
Wings of the spirit, gentle and kind.
With every heartbeat, a promise we weave,
In serene sanctuaries, we learn to believe.

The hush of the forest, the calm of the sea,
Nature's embrace sets our hearts free.
A place to reflect, to dream and grow,
In the haven of silence, His love we know.

Through trials and storms, we seek the grace,
In every struggle, a sacred space.
As clouds drift apart, light breaks the throng,
In serene sanctuaries, we find where we belong.

So let us gather in spirit and song,
In these sacred spaces, where we are strong.
Together united, our hearts all aglow,
Serene sanctuaries, where His blessings flow.

## Abiding in the Presence

In stillness deep, His voice we hear,
A gentle whisper, drawing near.
Light of the world, our hearts' pure song,
In His embrace, we all belong.

Through trials faced, with faith we rise,
His loving gaze, the endless skies.
In every moment, grace unfolds,
A sacred truth, His love beholds.

In shadows cast, His light breaks through,
With every breath, His promise true.
We walk by faith, our spirits soar,
Abiding here, forevermore.

In gratitude, our hearts now swell,
For in His arms, we know so well.
Each tear we shed, each joy we bring,
In His presence, our souls take wing.

Eternally held, our voices raise,
In harmony, we lift His praise.
A family bound by love divine,
In perfect peace, we intertwine.

## Names Written in Mercy

Within the book of life we find,
Each name inscribed, a heart aligned.
In mercy's grace, our flaws erased,
In love's embrace, we're gently traced.

Forgiven souls, we rise anew,
His endless love, forever true.
Restored in hope, through faith we stand,
With open hearts, He holds our hand.

In trials faced, our spirits grow,
Through darkest nights, His light will show.
We gather strength from love divine,
With each new dawn, our souls entwine.

A tapestry of grace we weave,
In unity, we choose to believe.
For every name, a story told,
In mercy's warmth, our hearts consoled.

Together bound by ties of grace,
We share the journey, every space.
With faith ignited, we seek the way,
In mercy's light, we choose to stay.

## The Anchor of Grace

In tempest's roar, we find our calm,
An anchor firm, a soothing balm.
With faith as strong as ocean's tide,
His grace is where our hearts abide.

Through stormy seas and winds that blow,
We trust in Him, our spirits grow.
In every trial, we're held close,
Anchored by love, that's what matters most.

When waves of doubt begin to rise,
We look above, toward the skies.
In quiet moments, hope restored,
His grace our refuge, forever adored.

Through every journey, hand in hand,
Together strong, we make our stand.
His promises, our charted course,
In grace we find our steady source.

Through valleys low, on mountaintops,
His grace abounds, it never stops.
An anchor sure, we shall embrace,
Forever held, in heaven's grace.

## The Essence of Belonging

In every heart, a place to rest,
Where love abounds, we feel the best.
In sacred bonds, our spirits meet,
The essence of belonging, sweet.

Together we rise, through thick and thin,
Bound as one, through loss and win.
Each voice a note, in harmony,
In faith we find our symphony.

Through shared joys and silent tears,
In every moment, conquering fears.
We gather strength from love's embrace,
The essence of belonging, grace.

Amidst the trials, we stand tall,
For in His love, we shall not fall.
With open hearts, we choose to sing,
The essence of belonging, a sacred thing.

Together we walk, hand in hand,
Through valleys deep and golden sand.
In every step, a purpose strong,
In love we find where we belong.

## Refuge in the Light

In shadows deep, I seek Thy face,
A guiding star, a sacred place.
With arms wide open, love like rain,
Thy gentle whisper soothes all pain.

When doubts arise, I lift my prayer,
In every breath, I feel Thee there.
The light that breaks the darkest night,
A refuge strong, my heart's delight.

In the stillness of the dawn's embrace,
I find my peace, my holy space.
Your promise clear as morning dew,
In every trial, I trust in You.

The path ahead, though steep and long,
With faith I walk, I sing my song.
The light will guide me through the fray,
In every step, I'll find my way.

At journey's end, a welcome home,
Where love abides, I'm never alone.
In refuge found, my spirit soars,
In light divine, I close the doors.

## The Warmth of Abiding Grace

In every moment, grace cascades,
A gentle touch in life's charades.
Through trials faced and burdens borne,
Your warmth envelops, hope reborn.

With heavy hearts, we seek the light,
In whispered prayers, both day and night.
Your tender mercy, a calming stream,
In every tear, we find the dream.

The hands that heal, the love that mends,
In unity, our spirit bends.
Through joy and sorrow, we share the day,
In boundless grace, we find our way.

The sun will rise, its golden hue,
As arms of grace wrap close 'round you.
In every trial, we stand embraced,
In hope and faith, forever laced.

In grateful hearts, Your love we trace,
In every moment, we find our place.
With open souls, we sing with glee,
In the warmth of grace, we are free.

## Where the Spirit Dwells

In quietude, where Spirit sings,
A sacred peace, the heart's soft wings.
Among the trees, in skies so blue,
The breath of life speaks pure and true.

In every heart that seeks to know,
The depths of grace, the rivers flow.
Through paths unknown, our souls unite,
In harmony, we share the light.

The spirit whispers through the night,
Guiding us home, a beacon bright.
In love's embrace, we learn to soar,
Together, we are evermore.

With open hands, we give and share,
Wherever we go, we find You there.
In each heartbeat, a prayer unfolds,
The spirit's warmth, a love that holds.

In every moment, grace descends,
A dance of souls, where love transcends.
Where the spirit dwells, we too abide,
A sacred bond, our hearts as one.

## **A Journey to the Beloved**

On paths unknown, our feet take flight,
In search of love, our guiding light.
With every step, a song we weave,
In whispered prayers, we dare believe.

Through valleys low and mountains high,
In every tear, a hopeful sigh.
The Beloved waits in fields of grace,
In tender moments, we find our place.

With open hearts, the journey calls,
In sacred spaces, the spirit falls.
Through trials faced and tempests loud,
We rise together, humble and proud.

In every bond, a sacred thread,
With courage strong, we forge ahead.
The love we seek, forever near,
In every heartbeat, You are here.

At journey's end, our spirits blend,
In love's embrace, we find our friend.
United souls, the Beloved's grace,
In every heart, we leave a trace.

## **Beneath the Celestial Canopy**

Under the stars, we gather in grace,
Silent hearts beat, in this holy space.
The moonlight shines on the weary soul,
Guiding our spirits, making us whole.

In the night's embrace, we find our peace,
Whispers of love that never cease.
Each twinkling light, a prayer that soars,
Connecting us all, across distant shores.

With faith as our anchor, we rise above,
Wrapped in the warmth of eternal love.
The vastness above, a promise divine,
In every heart, His light shall shine.

Together we stand, beneath the skies,
Hope ignites when the heart truly tries.
Here, in this moment, we feel Him near,
Beneath the canopy, we cast aside fear.

So we lift our voices, a humble refrain,
In the stillness, we break every chain.
Beneath the celestial, our spirits entwine,
For in His presence, true joy is a sign.

## **The Sacred Path Awaits**

Upon the path, illuminated bright,
With every step, we seek the light.
Guided by faith, our hearts inspire,
A journey of hope, kindled by fire.

Each moment taken, a gift profound,
In every stumble, His grace is found.
The sacred road, where love unfolds,
Teaching our hearts the truth it holds.

With hands united, we walk as one,
In this sacred space, we feel the sun.
The whispers of old, in each gentle breeze,
Invite us to walk, with hearts at ease.

For every trial, a lesson bestowed,
In the valley lows, our spirits are sowed.
The sacred path awaits our embrace,
Leading us forth to a holy place.

Side by side, we traverse the ways,
In love we find our eternal praise.
Each footstep taken, a promise made,
On this sacred path, never to fade.

## Whispered Prayers of Belonging

In the quiet night, whispers arise,
Carried on wings, to the endless skies.
Each prayer a thread, weaving us tight,
In the tapestry of love, hopeful and bright.

With every sigh, a wish to share,
A longing for grace, beyond compare.
In these whispered words, connection grows,
A bond of belonging, through highs and lows.

In the hearts of many, a song takes flight,
Breaking the silence, igniting the night.
We lift our voices to be heard,
In unity's strength, we find the word.

The circle of love, ever expanding,
In each gentle heart, a soft understanding.
Together we stand, a family intertwined,
In whispered prayers, our souls aligned.

For in this moment, we are enough,
In the presence of love, we rise above.
Whispered prayers, a sacred decree,
In the arms of grace, we are truly free.

## A Refuge in Sacred Tides

The ocean whispers, secrets untold,
Waves of compassion, forever bold.
In the ebb and flow, we find our peace,
A refuge in tides, where worries cease.

With each gentle wave, our burdens are shed,
In the salty air, our spirits are fed.
The rhythm of water, a soothing song,
In this sacred space, where we belong.

The horizon calls, offers hope anew,
Guiding our hearts to the vast and true.
In the depths of the sea, we seek our dreams,
As the sunlight dances, in golden beams.

Here in these waters, we find our trust,
In the sacred tides, we turn to dust.
Yet from this moment, we rise again,
In the circle of life, where love shall reign.

So we gather close, as the tides do rise,
In the embrace of the waves, hearts open wide.
A refuge in nature, where souls find home,
In the sacred tides, we are never alone.

## The Gift of Serenity

In quiet whispers, peace unfolds,
A promise made, as stillness holds.
In every breath, divinity,
A sanctuary for the weary soul.

From troubled waters, calm will rise,
In gentle grace, the heart complies.
With joy anew, the spirit sings,
In harmony with sacred things.

A light that shines in darkest night,
A beacon warm, a guiding sight.
Within each moment, love resides,
In prayerful thought, the heart abides.

Beneath the stars, we find our way,
In silent trust, we humbly pray.
The world may shift, but here remain,
The gift of peace, through joy and pain.

In humble gratitude, we stand,
With open hearts, and outstretched hand.
For every dawn, a new embrace,
The gift of serenity, our sacred place.

## Tree of Life and Light

In roots so deep, our spirits grow,
The tree of life, in light's warm glow.
Branches reach for skies above,
In every leaf, a tale of love.

With every season, strength we find,
In trials faced, our hearts aligned.
The sap of faith, it flows within,
A light that conquers all our sin.

Beneath the shade, we gather near,
In whispered prayers, our hopes sincere.
Encircled by the earth's embrace,
We seek the truth, we find our place.

As blossoms bloom, our souls they touch,
In unity, we're lifted much.
In every fruit, a promise born,
The tree of life, forever worn.

In light and love, we ever tread,
With gratitude, our spirits fed.
In harmony, we dance and sing,
The tree of life, our offering.

## Symphony of the Spheres

In cosmic dance, the spheres unite,
A symphony of love and light.
In harmony, the stars declare,
The sacred bond we all can share.

With every note, a prayer ascends,
Through time and space, where silence bends.
The universe in grand embrace,
A melody of boundless grace.

The whispers of the heavens sing,
In every heart, we feel the spring.
Together woven, souls entwined,
In sacred sound, our spirits aligned.

As planets spin and comets glide,
In rhythm true, love will abide.
With every breath, we are the song,
In unity, we all belong.

In this vast expanse, we find our role,
In every heartbeat, one shared soul.
The symphony, forever flows,
In light and love, the spirit grows.

## The Light of Home

In tranquil spaces, love resides,
A gentle glow, where peace abides.
The light of home, a warm embrace,
In humble corners, sacred space.

Through whispered dreams, our spirits soar,
In every heartbeat, we are more.
With family ties that gently bind,
In love's reflection, truth we find.

The laughter shared, the tears we shed,
Each moment cherished, softly spread.
In every shadow, hope will gleam,
In light of home, we find our dream.

In journeys far, we carry close,
The light of home, the heart's true pulse.
With gratitude, we walk this path,
In joy and sorrow, love will last.

In quiet nights, when all is still,
The light of home, it gently fills.
Forevermore, our hearts will roam,
In every sigh, we find our home.

## **Labyrinth of Lost Directions**

In shadows deep where whispers fade,
A wanderer's heart begins to stray.
Each turn conceals a guiding light,
Yet lost we feel, we yearn to pray.

O paths entwined in sacred time,
We seek the thread that leads us home.
Through echoes soft, our spirits climb,
In faith we rise, no more to roam.

With every step, the truth unfolds,
A map of love, divine and pure.
The heart unfolds, its secrets told,
In labyrinths, we find the cure.

The skies may weep, the storms may roar,
Yet deep within, the light will shine.
In every doubt, a truth ignites,
In every loss, the grace divine.

So wander on, O faithful soul,
In twisted paths, the heart shall soar.
For every step toward love's embrace,
Is finding Him, forevermore.

## The Grace of Returning Always

In silence deep, He calls us home,
Through winding roads, through fear and strife.
A gentle touch, the Spirit's grace,
Awakens hope, renewed in life.

The way may bend, the night may fall,
Yet in our hearts a spark remains.
A promise sung in whispered prayers,
To guide us through our earthly gains.

With arms wide open, love awaits,
No matter how far we may stray.
Each falter leads us to His side,
In every tear, a chance to pray.

So let the burdens softly fall,
And breathe in grace with every sigh.
For we are held, forever loved,
In every moment, we draw nigh.

As stars align, a path appears,
In darkness, light reveals the way.
We find our strength, we find our voice,
In grace, we learn to dance and sway.

## In Search of Celestial Anchors

When tempest tosses fragile hearts,
We search for steadfast guides above.
In every storm, our spirits bend,
Yet reach for anchors made of love.

The heavens speak in whispers clear,
Their constellations chart our dreams.
With faithful eyes, we trace the light,
In darkness, hope's bright beacon beams.

A sacred bond, celestial pull,
Connects our souls, entwined in prayer.
We rise as one, through doubt and fear,
In fervent faith, we learn to care.

For every star, a story told,
A history of love and grace.
In unity, we stand as one,
In search of truth, we find our place.

So cast your gaze upon the night,
And feel the warmth of love's embrace.
For we are bound by sacred ties,
In search of grace, we find our space.

## Nestled in the Light of Faith

In gentle dawn, the world awakes,
A canvas brushed with hues of gold.
We find our peace, as daylight breaks,
In whispered truths that are retold.

With every heartbeat, grace arrives,
A presence felt in morning's glow.
In quiet moments, love survives,
Nestled in faith, we learn to grow.

Each step we take, a holy ground,
In sacred rhythms, life unfolds.
With every breath, His joy is found,
A promise wrapped in warmth, consoled.

Through trials fierce, our spirits rise,
For in the storm, we know His name.
With eyes of hope, we claim the prize,
For faith ignites our hearts aflame.

So seek the light, embrace the truth,
For in His arms, we are made whole.
Nestled in faith, we find our youth,
In every prayer, a loving soul.

## Circles of Acceptance and Grace

In the heart of the gathering, we stand,
Threads of love connect every hand.
With open arms and spirits free,
We embrace the light, a divine decree.

In the circle of faith, we find our way,
Guided by love in bright array.
Each soul a spark, igniting the night,
Together we shine, in sacred light.

Through trials and joys, we learn to grow,
In acceptance deep, our spirits flow.
Bound by compassion, we rise above,
In circles entwined, we breathe pure love.

The grace we share, a gift so rare,
In every moment, felt everywhere.
With hearts aligned and voices strong,
We journey together, where we belong.

So let us gather, hand in hand,
In circles of grace, we take our stand.
With faith as our guide, we'll soar and dance,
In acceptance divine, we find our chance.

## The Tapestry of Sacred Memories

Woven by time, our stories unfold,
In threads of silver, moments bold.
Each memory a thread, shining bright,
In the tapestry of life, a sacred light.

Through laughter and tears, we find our peace,
In shared remembrance, our spirits cease.
Circles of family, friends, and grace,
In the heart's embrace, we find our place.

The fabric of love, so pure and true,
Stitched together by me and you.
In every stitch, a whisper of prayer,
In the tapestry of life, our hearts lay bare.

As seasons change, the colors blend,
In the sacred weaving, we transcend.
Each moment cherished, a story retold,
In the tapestry of memories, we behold.

So let us gather, in warmth and light,
To cherish the moments that feel so right.
For in this tapestry, we find our way,
In the sacred threads of every day.

**A Sojourn Towards Our Roots**

Beneath the ancient trees, we wander slow,
Tracing the paths where wise winds blow.
In each leaf's rustle, a story twined,
Unfolding the wisdom of the divine.

With every step, our spirits align,
As we seek the roots, our souls entwine.
The soil, a cradle of sacred grace,
Nurtures the hearts in this hallowed place.

Echoes of ancestors whisper near,
In the gentle breeze, their love we hear.
A sojourn of faith, a pilgrimage true,
In seeking our roots, we find something new.

As seasons shift and time moves on,
We honor the past, where we've all come from.
In the embrace of the earth, we are one,
In the journey of life, our search begun.

So let us walk, in reverent stride,
Towards our roots, with hearts open wide.
For in every step, we learn to see,
The beauty of love, of unity.

## **Enchanted by the Familiar**

In the warmth of the hearth, we gather close,
The laughter and stories, like sweet prose.
In familiar faces, the love we trace,
An enchantment dwells in this sacred space.

Each moment we share, a treasure, a gift,
In the dance of the familiar, our spirits lift.
With hands held tightly, we journey as one,
Enchanted by life, beneath the sun.

Through the heart's embrace, connections grow,
In simplicity's beauty, our spirits flow.
The comfort of home, where we belong,
In familiar rhythms, we sing our song.

As stars ignite in the velvet night,
We find solace together, our hearts alight.
In the gentle whisper of love's sweet call,
We dwell in the familiar, embraced by all.

So let us cherish the ties that bind,
In the familiar warmth, our souls aligned.
For in this enchantment, we see the grace,
Of love's deep roots in a sacred place.

## Sacred Ground

Beneath the sky, the earth does glow,
In whispers soft, the spirits flow.
A place where grace and mercy meet,
Our hearts are grounded, pure, and sweet.

With every step, we tread with care,
In holy hush, we find our prayer.
The ancient trees stand strong and tall,
They weave a life that stirs our call.

Through trials faced, our souls ignite,
In sacred ground, we seek the light.
The path of love, it leads us home,
In every heart, the seeds are sown.

The songs of old fill up the air,
In harmony, we share our share.
The binding threads of faith entwine,
In every moment, we align.

Come walk with me, let's raise our voice,
In faith and hope, we now rejoice.
On sacred ground, our spirits soar,
In unity, forevermore.

## The Echo of Faithful Footsteps

In silence deep, the echoes ring,
Of faithful hearts, our praises sing.
Each step we take, a story told,
Of love divine, of faith and bold.

Through valleys low and mountains high,
We walk in faith, we touch the sky.
The footprints left, a trail of grace,
In every heart, a sacred space.

The whispers soft, they guide our way,
In darkest night, they bring the day.
With every breath, we seek the truth,
In every step, we find our youth.

The echoes linger through the years,
A chorus formed of joy and tears.
In unity, our spirits blend,
Through faithful paths, our steps descend.

Together now, we rise anew,
In every heart, a vision true.
The echo calls, and we abide,
In faithful footsteps, side by side.

## Embracing the Everlasting

In quiet dawn, a promise wakes,
The love we hold, no fear, no breaks.
Embracing now, the ever pure,
In faith's embrace, our hearts endure.

With open arms, we greet the day,
In every word, we find our way.
The everlasting truth we seek,
In gentle strength, we rise, not weak.

The sun shall shine upon our soul,
In every moment, we are whole.
Through trials fierce, we stand our ground,
In love's embrace, we are unbound.

As seasons change, our spirits grow,
In every heart, the grace will flow.
Embracing all, the joy and pain,
In every tear, the love remains.

Together here, we find our place,
In unity, we seek His grace.
Embracing now, the light we share,
In everlasting love, we care.

## Wanderer's Prayer

Oh path unknown, I search for light,
In wanderer's heart, there's hope in sight.
With every step, my soul takes flight,
  In gentle whispers, I find my might.

Guide me, Lord, through trials and pain,
  In fleeting joy and dancing rain.
The heart of wanderer, pure and free,
  In every moment, I long to be.

With stars above, a map to chart,
  A journey led by faith's own heart.
In every shadow, grace I find,
  A love unbroken, free, and kind.

As I roam through fields of grace,
  I seek the truth in every place.
In wonder's grasp, I listen near,
For every prayer, I hold so dear.

So hear my plea, through valleys wide,
  In every step, be by my side.
Oh wanderer's prayer, I humbly say,
  Guide my heart along the way.

## The Graceful Return

In shadows deep, the lost are led,
By gentle hands, where angels tread.
With open arms, they find their way,
To light restored, the break of day.

A whisper soft, through darkness calls,
The heart awakens, as mercy falls.
Through trials faced, their spirits yearn,
In faith and hope, they always learn.

With every step, redemption's near,
Guided by love, they shed their fear.
Each tear is caught, a gift of grace,
In sacred time, they find their place.

The road is long, but never lost,
For every gain comes without cost.
In silent prayers, their burdens shared,
The grace bestowed, divinely cared.

So let them rise, the humble souls,
Embraced by love, they feel made whole.
In sacred circles, joy returns,
With every heart, the spirit burns.

## Sheltered by Mercy

Upon the mount, where shadows fade,
 In quiet grace, our hearts are laid.
 Beneath the veil of endless skies,
We seek the truth, where wisdom lies.

With open hearts, we humbly pray,
 For mercy's light to guide our way.
 In every trial, we find our peace,
 A shelter built, where fears may cease.

Through storms that rage, we stand as one,
 In faith we rise, beneath the sun.
 With every tear, a seed is sown,
 And in that soil, our love has grown.

Each gentle breeze, a whispered song,
 Reminds us here where we belong.
 In every soul, a spark divine,
 United strong, our hearts align.

So let us walk, on paths of grace,
 With mercy's arms, a warm embrace.
 In love we dwell, forever free,
 In sacred bonds, eternally.

## **The Heart's Holy Place**

In quiet chambers, hearts reside,
Where whispers soft, like ocean tide.
In sacred stillness, spirit flows,
With every breath, the presence grows.

A gentle light, within us burns,
With every prayer, the heart now yearns.
In love's reflection, souls ignite,
In endless grace, we find our sight.

With humble hearts, we offer praise,
In gratitude, our voices raise.
Each note a prayer, a song divine,
In every moment, His love we find.

Through trials faced, we stand our ground,
In faith's embrace, our strength is found.
In every heartbeat, His will we seek,
In silent trust, we find the meek.

So let us cherish, this sacred space,
Where love abounds, in endless grace.
With open hearts, we come to hold,
The holy warmth, of love untold.

## **Echoes of Eternal Love**

In twilight's hush, the echoes call,
Of sacred love that binds us all.
Through valleys low and mountains high,
In every soul, the spirit flies.

With every prayer, our hearts align,
In unity, the stars entwine.
With every word, a promise made,
In love's embrace, we shun the shade.

The stories shared, of grace profound,
In laughter sweet, our hearts unbound.
In every tear, a lesson learned,
In every joy, our spirits turned.

A journey vast, through time and space,
In every moment, we find His face.
With grateful hearts, we sing His song,
In echo's dance, we all belong.

So let us walk, in faith and light,
With love as guide, we take our flight.
In timeless grace, forever true,
The echoes ring, in me and you.

## **Whispers of the Sacred**

In silence, faith begins to bloom,
Hearts entwined in sacred room.
Whispers soft upon the breeze,
Calling souls with gentle ease.

The stars above, a guiding light,
Their shimmer brings the darkest night.
In prayer we find our spirits soar,
United in the evermore.

Each moment wrapped in love divine,
In every breath, the holy sign.
Nature sings, its praise unfolds,
A symphony of stories told.

With gratitude, our voices rise,
To touch the heavens, to the skies.
In every heart, the light aglow,
A promise made, forever flow.

So let us walk this hallowed ground,
In sacred whispers, hope is found.
For in the stillness, we shall know,
The truth of love, the sacred flow.

## **The Beacon of Belonging**

In the midst of shadows cast,
A beacon shines, a light steadfast.
With open arms and heart so wide,
We find our solace, where love abides.

Through trials faced and storms we brave,
Together bound, our spirits save.
In unity, our voices blend,
A sacred bond that will not end.

Each soul a thread, a vibrant hue,
In tapestry, life we pursue.
The warmth of kindness fills the air,
A gift of grace, our hearts laid bare.

In every laugh and tear we share,
The essence of our love laid bare.
As one we stand, in truth, we grow,
In this embrace, our spirits flow.

So let us shine, a guiding spark,
Through darkest nights, we leave a mark.
With faith as anchor, we belong,
A family forged, forever strong.

## An Offering of the Heart

In the stillness, prayers arise,
An offering shared beneath the skies.
With every whisper, every sigh,
The heart extends, a love supply.

In humble ways, we seek to share,
The light within, a faithful prayer.
Each act of kindness, gentle grace,
Lifts weary souls to a sacred place.

Like blooming flowers, souls unfold,
In beauty wrapped, our stories told.
With gratitude, we take our part,
To share the love, an open heart.

Through trials faced, our spirits blend,
In every heart, a sacred friend.
Together journeyed, hand in hand,
In love's embrace, forever stand.

So let this offering take flight,
A gift of love, pure and bright.
In every moment, let us see,
The heart's true path to harmony.

## The Nurturing Light

In twilight's hush, the light appears,
A guiding star to calm our fears.
With gentle touch, it warms the soul,
In every heart, it makes us whole.

Through winding paths, it leads the way,
A sacred flame that will not sway.
Each step we take, it shines so clear,
A nurturing light, forever near.

In the garden where kindness grows,
The seeds of faith, our hearts expose.
As blossoms burst, we find our place,
In nature's arms, a warm embrace.

Together, let us kindle flame,
In every heart, we find the same.
In every moment, freely share,
The light of love, a true repair.

So let us walk with hearts alight,
In unity, we feel the might.
A nurturing light, forever bright,
Awakens joy, dispels the night.

## In the Bosom of the Divine

In quiet dawn, the spirit sings,
A whisper from the heart of things.
With every breath, a prayer ascends,
In love's embrace, where grace transcends.

In shadows cast by earthly strife,
The light divine ignites our life.
Through trials fierce, His hand will guide,
In faith, we walk, with Him beside.

Blessed are those who seek His face,
In every moment, find His grace.
With humble hearts, we rise and bow,
In the bosom, we find our vow.

Eternal love, our souls align,
In every heart, His light does shine.
O sacred bond, unbroken thread,
In Him alone, we'll find our bed.

As heavens vast, our voices blend,
Together we, on Him depend.
In the silence, hear His call,
In the bosom, we find our all.

## Sheltering Within Sacred Walls

Within these walls, our stories weave,
A refuge found, we dare believe.
In every stone, a prayer resides,
In unity, our faith abides.

The windows glow with sacred light,
Each beam a whisper of the night.
With open arms, the spirit sways,
In sacredness, our souls embrace.

From ancient tales, our hearts shall learn,
In every corner, candles burn.
The echoes of our voices blend,
In worship sweet, our souls ascend.

Together here, we face the storm,
In sacred walls, our hearts are warm.
Through trials fierce, we find our peace,
In love's embrace, all fears will cease.

As generations gather round,
In stories shared, our faith is found.
Beneath the arch, in trust we stand,
Within these walls, His guiding hand.

## An Odyssean Prayer for Rest

On distant shores, my heart does roam,
In restless waves, I seek my home.
With weary feet and eyes so dim,
I raise my voice, my prayer to Him.

In night's embrace, the stars above,
Whisper softly of endless love.
A tide that lifts, a current strong,
In faith, I linger, where I belong.

O guide me to the shores of peace,
Where sorrow fades and troubles cease.
In every wave, a gentle sigh,
An odyssean wish to fly.

Let not the storms of life dismay,
With open heart, I find the way.
In tranquil depths, my spirit rests,
In prayer, I seek the soul's behest.

So grant me peace, O Lord of grace,
In every journey, Your warm embrace.
As I traverse this winding quest,
I find my hope, my heart at rest.

# The Embrace of Generations Past

In whispers soft, the ancients speak,
Through time and space, their wisdom's sleek.
We carry forth their dreams and prayers,
In every heart, their love declares.

The roots so deep, from where we came,
Inherit strength, in love's great name.
With open hands, we share the light,
In living truth, they shine so bright.

Each cherished moment, honor's grace,
In every smile, we find their trace.
Through trials faced, their courage steeped,
In faith's embrace, we've truly leaped.

The stories told around the fire,
In every soul, ignite desire.
Together bound, we walk the path,
In gratitude, we share their wrath.

For every lesson that they've shared,
A legacy of love declared.
The embrace of generations past,
In future hearts, their love will last.

## The Illuminated Path Home

In shadows deep, the light shall gleam,
A guiding star, a whispered dream.
With every step, our hearts ignite,
The path to peace, our souls take flight.

With faith as compass, love our guide,
In every tear, He'll be our pride.
We walk together, hand in hand,
Towards the promise of His land.

In quiet moments, prayers unfold,
For every heart, His grace be told.
The journey long, yet hope endures,
In sacred trust, our spirits soar.

Beneath the stars, in night so calm,
We find our spirits, healed and warm.
His mercy flows, a gentle stream,
Awakening our heart's true dream.

Through trials faced, we rise anew,
In every struggle, we see what's true.
In unity, our voices blend,
A hymn of love that has no end.

## Celestial Refuge

In whispers soft, the heavens sigh,
A shelter found, where spirits fly.
Each prayer we send, like stars above,
In boundless grace, we feel His love.

The storms may rage, the night may fall,
Yet in His arms, we stand so tall.
With open hearts, we seek His face,
In every moment, we find grace.

As light descends, a warm embrace,
Through trials faced, we know His space.
In faith, united, strong we stand,
A tribute to His guiding hand.

With every tear, He makes us whole,
In whispered prayers, we touch our soul.
With every dawn, His light resounds,
In sacred silence, love abounds.

A refuge found in trust divine,
In every heartbeat, love we find.
Together bound, in joy we sing,
A melody of hope, our offering.

## Sheltered by Love

Within His arms, we find our place,
For love surrounds, a warm embrace.
In every trial, His promise stands,
A fortress built by holy hands.

When shadows fall, and fears arise,
We lift our hearts, we seek the skies.
With every breath, we find our way,
A journey blessed, come what may.

In gentle whispers, truth is shared,
In sacred moments, souls are bared.
With hope restored, our spirits soar,
In love's sweet arms, we are reborn.

Through valleys low and mountains high,
With trust, we rise and never die.
His light will guide, our hearts will mend,
A journey wrapped in love, transcends.

Together we walk, in faith's embrace,
A timeless bond, our rightful place.
In every heartbeat, His love we trace,
Sheltered by love, we find our grace.

## The Sanctuary of Grace

In sacred stillness, we abide,
With open hearts, our souls collide.
Here in the quiet, peace descends,
A refuge found, where love transcends.

Through trials faced, His hand we seek,
In every moment, strong yet meek.
With faith as anchor, hope our song,
In grace's arms, we all belong.

With every prayer, the walls will rise,
A sanctuary where spirits prize.
His mercy flows in gentle streams,
Reflecting all our hidden dreams.

In unity, we gather near,
With hearts entwined, we cast out fear.
Together strong, our voices blend,
In harmony, the love won't end.

Our sanctuary, a blessed space,
Where every soul finds endless grace.
In faith we stand, in love we grow,
A sacred light, forever glow.

Milton Keynes UK
Ingram Content Group UK Ltd.
UKHW050411091224
451733UK00025B/110